Things I wish I knew before moving to *Paris*

100+ Quick Tips for Your Life in Paris

a quick guide by Kiana Tiese

A quick forward:

I remember looking out the window during my first cab ride in Paris and thinking, is this it? I'd spent my pre-teen years watching *The Hills* and knowing that "Paris is always a good idea,". In fact, everything I knew about Paris was fed to me through television and magazines in a glamorized *"Gichee-Gichee-Ya-Ya-ch-cha"* kinda way.

I'd landed in Charles De Gaulle airport wearing as many layers of clothing as I could to keep my suitcase from costing extra, a student visa, and no return ticket. I stuck my head out the window hoping to see the Eiffel Tower. Instead, I found myself staring out the window as we drove through the 18th arrondissement to Guy Môquet wondering why Blair and Serena had never gone shopping over here.

I quickly fell in love with the neighborhood, the city itself, and of course, a few Frenchmen. I had no idea how long I would be staying in Paris or how I would make it work but I remained up to the challenge. My transformation from a tourist to an expat was not linear; there were moments of wondering if I should just go home and where 'home' even was at this point.

This guide is what I should've been reading during those first few months in Paris instead of swiping left and right and sipping cheap wine. It's a mix of both practical and social tips, that may fill in some blanks about moving to (or visiting) Paris, draw some inspiration, and/or give you a little laugh.

I genuinely hope it does all three.

Paris, 2017

My first few days in Paris vs. my first appointment at the Prefecture

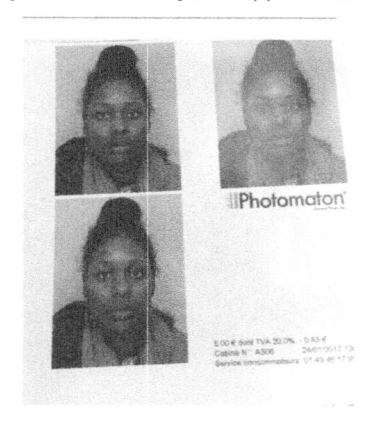

So you want to move to or visit Paris?

Here's what you should know.

---

1. Size matters
2. The Hills are Alive
3. Pay or Pray
4. Don't Get Robbed
5. About That Paper
6. Wait Time
7. English is Everywhere
8. First Week French
9. Say Hello
10. Call Me Beep Me
11. Charming Isn't Cute
12. Penthouse Suite
13. Get in on the Ground
14. Hott in Hurr
15. Summer Time
16. Time to Eat
17. What to Eat + When
18. Picnics
19. Pineapples and Peaches
20. Apéros
21. Recettes
22. What to Say
23. Shop till You Drop
24. Shop Somemore
25. Dates
26. Double Dates
27. Sick Days
28. Teach and Learn
29. Learn French
30. Fundamental French
31. Networks
32. Scam and the City
33. Emily Forgot

Paris is Small

That means you can get across the city in an hour or less (by metro).

That also means you may run into that ex you're avoiding.

Bring good walking sneakers because walking the city is the best way to get around.

Lots of people use alternate transportation such as Velib bikes that cost less than 5.00 per month.

The Hills are Alive

This is a hilly city filled with cobblestone streets and stairs.

Many sidewalks are small or have active construction happening.

Metro stations like 'Abbesses' or tourist attraction Sacré-Cœur Basilica are stair heavy so, be prepared (or take the elevator).

This means Paris is not very accessible for the handicapped and/or elderly.

Pay or Pray

If you do take the metro please pay or pray.

Either, pay 1.87 for a single ticket (and save it until you have exited your destination station) or, pray that you don't run into the 'Controllers'.

These (green uniform) wearing people may be waiting around the corner or enter the bus or train car when you least expect it. If you run into them without a ticket be prepared to pay a fine (35.00 and up).

Sadly, not knowing this rule or not speaking French can't save you.

Don't get Robbed

The metros are pickpocket heaven. Be extra cautious and aware of your surroundings when you take the metro. This means:

- Do not speak English loudly (you will draw attention to yourself, this is how I got pickpocketed).

- Keep your phone and wallet in your (closed) bag

- Don't hold your phone loosely in your hands (especially if you're sitting by the door).

About That Paper

You will need originals and to make copies of everything you own.

That also means you may become a hoarder (better safe than sorry)!

Apostille: You attach this to your original document to verify it is legitimate and authentic.

Translations: Documents like birth certificates will need to be translated by an official translator. Rates usually start around €50.00.

Notarize: Important documents may need to be notarized in France to prove their authenticity. Check your embassy website first before calling a Notaire up (they do more real-estate and estate-planning transactions than stamping paperwork).

The Only Thing That Goes Fast in France is the Wine

You will have to adjust your expectations for responses, approvals, or things being finished. You will need to wait for an appointment then, send the paperwork over via mail, then resend when the copies are inevitably lost.

Get used to following up over the phone, via email, and in-person if you need an answer to something urgent.

There is no shame in asking your French friends (or any native French speaker that you may know) to accompany you or make phone calls on your behalf. Native French speakers are taken more seriously and having an accent may add to your wait time.

English is everywhere*

That means that you may be able to find a job speaking English with an International company or use this skill to create your own job.

That also means that French people may automatically switch to English when they hear your accent in French.

Being a native English speaker can be a huge advantage. I used this to tutor English although I had little experience.

*This does not mean you shouldn't learn the basics before coming.

First week French

Those first few days in Paris may be overwhelming, especially if you aren't familiar with basic French.

Here are some words and phrases that will help you regardless of your itinerary :

- Je voudrais (juh voodray) : I would like
- Sortie : exit
- Est-ce-que-vous parlez anglais (eskuh voo parlay ahnglay) : Do you speak English?
- Le prix (luh pree) : the price
- S'il vous plaît (silvoo play) : please
- Où sont les toilettes (oo son les toilets) : where is the bathroom
- L'addition : the bill
- Je cherche (juh church) : I am searching for...

Say Hello!

When entering any shop (even if you don't see the attendant there). This rule also applies when entering a bus or taxi.

Always air on the side of formality and politeness when dealing with French people. Politesse is expected in all situations.

Before asking a question, be sure to say hello first. Saying 'sorry' or 'excuse me' and then jumping into your question is not acceptable here.

Formal = Bonjour
Less formal= Salut
Very familiar = Coucou
Whats up = Ça Va

Call me ! Beep me!

The main phone providers in France are Orange, SFR, Bouygues, and Free.

My phone plan with unlimited data costs about 20.00 a month.

Most cell phone numbers start with 06 or 07 and are written in this format : 06 59 17 99 99.

Most office phone numbers start with 01.

If you want to end your phone contract you will need to send a registered letter (lettre commandée) to the company formally asking to have your phone cut off.

When setting up a phone plan and sim card you will need a credit/debit card and proof of address.

'Charming' isn't Cute

If you see the words 'charming' or 'cozy' on an apartment listing this is code for small. Very small.

'Charming' tiny apartments are the norm in Paris so be prepared to downsize when moving.

If the apartment ad shows pictures of stairs that means there isn't an elevator.

Meuble: furnished
Non-Meuble: unfurnished
WC: Toilets
WC sur Palier: Shared toilet in the hallway
Lumineux: luminous, light-filled

Penthouse Suites

The top floor in most Parisian apartments is not the penthouse suites you'd imagine. The top floor historically has been reserved for maids' rooms.

Chambre de bonne rooms start at 9m2 . These apartments are usually on the top floor, under the roof, without elevators.

Rent should be cheaper in these 'apartments' ranging from 300-900 EUR per month.

I paid 520.00 for a 16m2 apartment in Paris 75011.

Sites to find apartment leads include: Seloger, PAP and cartedecoloc.fr.

You will need a 'dossier' and French garants to apply for apartments. Many landlords want you to be making 3x the rental price for approval.

Get in on the Ground Level

The first floor is what we would consider the second floor in the US.

The ground floor is called RDC or Rez-de-chaussée , right above that is the first floor, and so on. The basement is called the 'cave' (pronounced like calve).

Guardiennes and Concierges are usually on the ground floors of buildings.

There may be Doctor's offices mixed with residential offices in some buildings. The office will say which building and floor it is located on.

Hott in hurr

Get ready to adjust to the celcius system where 19°C is a heatwave whereas in the States it's freezing cold.

There are heatwaves each summer in Paris that can last weeks at a time. Be prepared by:

- Buying a tiny fan or small AC unit

- Hanging AC units are usually banned unless approved by the building

- Avoid your apartment during the day (most people spend hot summer days at cafes)

- Glaçons are ice cubes; ask for ice with your water (don't assume it will be served with ice)

Summer, Summer, Summer, Time

American tourists tend to come to Paris in the summer but, the city is practically empty!

Most shops (not including large chains) are closed either in July or August with nothing but a handwritten sign announcing their vacation.

Most Parisians leave the city in the summer to escape to the countryside or beach.

If you happen to be in Paris in the summer, try cooling off at:

- Paris Plages (outdoor beach set up on the Seine river and in the 19th near Vilette Canal Basin)

- Swimming pools like 'Piscine Georges Hermant'

- You will need a swimming cap and to take a shower before entering the pool.

- Most women wear one-pieces at public pools and men wear clinging swimming trunks.

Time to Eat

Paris is known for its cafés and terraces. In a time before COVID-19, you could go sit at a cafe and pay for a coffee (1.20 euros), sit, and watch the world go by.

You can spend money on expensive restaurants with Eiffel Tower views or you can go to local Brasseries or Bistrots. Street food is also a good bet - it all depends on where you are and your budget.

I always suggest trying the plât du jour at local brasseries, this is made fresh and inspired by the chef that day. I am biased, but the best restaurants for local and street food are in the 11th arrondissement.

Lunch is served in restaurants from 11:30-15h usually. I can't count how many times I wanted a late lunch at 4:30 only to find the restaurant was closed until dinner.

I have a lunch break from 12:30-2 pm, most people take long lunch breaks in corporate environments.

What to Eat and When

There are seasonal foods French people eat such as Raclette and Fondue. These two kinds of specialty cheeses are mainly eaten in the winter and in group settings.

Raclette parties are meant to be had with groups of friends who each bring things such as raclette cheese (flavors like smoked, pepper, truffle, etc.) a raclette machine, salad, cooked potatoes, crudités, charcuterie meat, and of course, wine.

One of my favorite fondue restaurants in Paris is called *Pain Vin Fromage*; the menu is in the name, bread, wine, and cheese!

Picnics

As soon as the weather gets warm, people are outside picnicking.

Always bring at least one drink, one snack, and one fruit. You can get all* of these at a local supermarket.

*Alcohol isn't sold in supermarkets after 10pm nor on Sundays.

Someone is always going to forget to bring cups and a bottle opener. Plan ahead and save the day (or ask the people next to you and make new friends).

Pinneapples vs Peaches

A Parisian once told me,

> "French people are like pineapples, tough on the outside but soft on the inside. Americans are like peaches, soft on the outside but hard on the inside,".

I have found that making friends in Paris can be challenging because many Parisians have their own close-knit group that they have known for decades.

Even if you speak French, you may not have the same cultural references as French people thus, making it harder to relate.

Try not to fall into the trap of being the "foreign friend" amongst your French friends.

Insist that they speak French with you!

Aperos

French people love apéros (what we would consider 'happy hour').

These are super informal, casual gatherings surrounding catching up over wine, beer, or light drinks (Apérol spritz, anyone?)

If you're ever invited to an apéro, similar to a picnic, do not come empty-handed or early! Bring a bottle of something, cheese, bread, or small finger foods. There are sections in the grocery store with apéro-friendly foods.

At my last apéro, I made stuffed mushrooms and bacon-wrapped dates. Both simple to make and go fast!

Recettes

Stuffed Mushrooms
- Preheat your oven to 170°C or 350°F
- Begin to clean and dry your mushrooms. You can use a moist paper towel for this part.
- Take out the stems of your mushrooms and chop them into small chunks.
  - Save the mushroom caps.
  - I suggest putting them on a non-stick pan and into the oven while you work on the next part. This will remove some of the moisture.
- Melt your oil or butter in a skillet over a medium heat and add minced garlic.
- Once the garlic starts to cook, you add your chopped mushrooms.
- Season the mixture with Italian seasoning, salt, and pepper to your liking.
- Once the mushrooms and garlic have cooked down, take them out of the skillet and allow to cool a bit.
- In a separate bowl, begin to mix the mushroom garlic combination with your cream cheese, and Parmesan cheese. You can taste and adjust for seasoning as well.
  - You can always add a bit of spice with cayenne or paprika depending on your taste
  - You can also add chopped crab meat, if you fancy.
- Begin to scoop your cream cheese mixture into your mushroom caps and top with more Parmesan and a bit of standard bread crumbs for crunch.
- Place in oven and let bake for around *20 minutes.
  - *This depends on how much moisture you'd like in your mushrooms. If you've already begun baking the caps then there should already be some liquid under the caps. You want to discard this liquid before stuffing and baking the mushrooms again.
- Remove and garnish with parsley.

Bonus: Mouth-watering cheesy-mushroom baguette
- Take your excess cheese and mushroom mixture and spread this on a cut baguette. Top with any remaining cheese and toast in the oven for about 10 min. It may seem strange but this mushroom-y bread goes just as fast as the mushrooms themselves and it's easy to make!

Grocery list

- Soft Cream Cheese (1.95 for a large tub of Madame Loik)
- A package of whole, fresh mushrooms (.99 eu)
- Minced garlic
- Italian Seasoning (Knorr Secrets d'Arome Plein Sud is a must)
- Parsley (for garnish)
- Salt and Pepper to taste
- Parmesan Cheese (1.00 eu for a grated bag)
- Bread crumbs
- Olive oil or Butter
- Fresh Baguette (1.00 eu for a full, .50 for a half)
- Whole dates (5.00 eu for a pack)
- Smoked Paprika
- Bacon (Thin cut, American style may be hard to find. Check Franprix and Marks and Spencers)
- Soft Cream Cheese
- Salt and Pepper to taste
- Toothpicks

Stuffed Dates
This one is also easy, but removing the date pits is a labor of love!
- Preheat your oven to 170°C or 350°F.
- Cut each date in half and remove pit. Place aside.
  - I would suggest wearing gloves as it can get sticky
- In a bowl, season soft cream cheese with smoked paprika, salt and pepper to your taste.
- You can use a bit of cayenne, but don't get crazy.
- Spoon the cream cheese mixture into the dates, careful not to overstuff.
- Take your thinly sliced bacon and cut each strip in half to make shorter strips.
- Wrap each date with one half of a bacon strip. Use a toothpick to hold the bacon and date together.
- You will most likely have more dates than bacon. Consider this a vegetarian-friendly option and stuff the remaining dates with the cream cheese.
- Place dates on a non-stick pan toothpicks width apart. Bake for about 20 min or until bacon looks crispy and you want to taste!

What to say

French people drink and talk about all types of things. Unlike Americans, topics like politics are not off the table for the French.

Growing up, I was told never to talk about religion, sex, or politics but all of those topics are on the table here.

The French (Parisians) also like to complain and are generally blasé about things so don't expect a lot of 'awesome' or 'OMG'!!

There's a certain type of humor French people love to use: Second Degré. This gives them the freedom to say whatever they want under the guise of humor.

Shop 'till You Drop

There are big supermarket chains where you can do your grocery shopping including Frankprix, Carrefour, Auchon, LIDL, etc.

Plastic bags are less and less common in Paris.

You can also do your grocery shopping at outdoor markets; each neighborhood has biweekly markets. Bring cash and a tote bag for these.

Traitors sell pre-made specialty foods such as Italian, Greek, Chinese, etc.

Shop Some More

For housing goods and knick-knacks, check out Brocantes. These are outdoor fleamarkets usually done on Weekends. The biggest one is called Les puces de Saint-Ouen.

You can find when and where the local brocantes are online at vide-greniers.org.

For housing decor, visit Emmaüs.

For second-hand shopping see 'Vide-Dressings'. This translates into 'Empty closets'. Men and Women will set up racks of their clothes to sell in their apartments, at bars, or other indoor venues. They may also sell their clothes at Brocantes.

Kilo shops are thrift stores located around the city where you choose your clothes and pay by weight.

Stop by Chinemachine in Montmarte and Bis Boutique Solidaire in the 11th arrondissement.

Dates

The date and time are written differently in France.

The date format is :
DAY/MONTH/YEAR
The time format is : Xh (h is for hour)

The time format is military time. One trick to converting is last digit minus two.

16h (last digit is 6) - 2 = 4pm

Do not expect French people to be on time for drinks or dinner, always account for 15 minutes or so.

Double Dates

Dating Frenchmen deserves its own guide...maybe one day ;).

For me, here is how it usually goes down:

- French men are more in touch with their emotions and unafraid to make bold declarations of love

- French men may decide that after the first kiss, you two are exclusively dating

- They also may be 'over it' within the month

- Lots of Parisians cohabitate early on

- A lot of Parisians have their small groups of friends which may include a few friendly exes

Sick days

The best way to make a doctor's appointment is through the website Doctolib.fr.

If you don't have a health care card you can pay cash or by card. The costs can start at 25.00 and range depending on the type of doctor. Most list their prices on the Doctolib site.

Doctors on this site will often list that they speak English - still, keep your expectations low.

If you need basic medicine you can go to pharmacies and ask for help. Pharmacies in tourist areas usually have an English speaker on staff. There is a late-night pharmacy near metro Republic.

If you need to get tested, check out 'centre de depistage'.

Teach and learn

A very common job for English speakers is teaching English in France. You can do this at a school, privately, or online for numerous companies.

There's the TAPIF visa that allows you to teach English at the Elementary and Secondary level part-time all over France.

Teaching privately means setting your own price, finding clients, and sporadic hours (cancellations can happen at any time). Most of these gigs are word of mouth, look for postings at Language schools, Universities, Facebook groups, and apps like SuperProf.

Online classes can include teaching English to students all over the world at random hours. There are tons of websites looking for Native speakers.

Learn French

I've been learning French since I landed at Charles de Gaulle. One of my favorite things about my life here is the option to learn and improve in French daily. There comes a point in your learning process where things just click. That is one of the best feelings!

I've been in Paris for four years and I've finally stopped beating myself up for not being fluent in French. I've made some strides but sometimes, I feel like I've hit a plateau.

I have to remind myself that there are multiple levels to learning French: speaking, writing, reading, listening, and understanding which all take time to grab.

The class I'm currently is taught by someone you may know (my friend in my head): Damon Dominique! He's the ultimate American in Paris Youtuber and he understands how we learn French as foreigners so I like his methodology. Plus he's funny as hell. If you want, I have a signup code for his class.

Fundamental French

Here are the other things I've done to improve my French level:

- Taking intensive courses (I did at Sorbonne CCFS and Campus Langues),

- Watching TV shows (I love Les Reines du Shopping),

- Watching movies in French with English subtitles,

- Listening to popular French music artists (all hail the Queens Aya and Angèle),

- Reading children's books and watching children's shows.

Networks

Be sure to join Facebook groups and Real life groups for expats in order to meet and connect with other expats. Some that I like are :

Expats in Paris and Suburbs
Wanted Community Paris
Americans in France
Expats in France
Women in Paris
Anti-Racists in Paris
WICE
American Church in Paris (I found my apartment listed outside their church)

Scam and the City

Please never send anyone money for services promising you to set up your visa or housing. Or, if you do, just do thorough research first.

If you need to change visa types ex: Au Pair into Student Visa, you will most likely need to do this at home at your Consulate. If you need to renew a visa you will most likely need to do this locally at the Prefecture.

If the apartment owner is 'abroad' and needs you to wire them money to secure your visit it's a scam. You will never need to pay to visit an apartment.

Do not hand over money until you have your (working) key to the apartment.

Do not sign any paperwork by groups of women asking you to donate.

Do not click links to pay anything if the number starts with 07

Do not play any street games involving cups and money (found in mostly tourist areas), they're rigged!

Emily Forgot

There are things you may experience in Paris that you did not expect to have to deal with such as bigotry, racial profiling, sexism, racism, xenophobia, etc. Try to keep an open mind and realistic expectations about living in a large city and the good and bad that comes with that.

Moving to a new country can be harder than you anticipated. If you ever feel like you need help just reach out to one of the above networks. There is no shame in looking for new friends in your neighborhood to go on a walk with or just comisserate with about life in France.

Take off your *Emily in Paris* rose-colored glasses and stay grounded in reality. Paris is great but it is not perfect nor is it an escape from whoever you are and whatever your problems may be back home.

Be ready to change and grow in ways your friends back home may not understand. That's ok, you didn't move to Paris to stay the same.

A *Quick* Thank-You:

Thank you to all my friends who became family here in Paris. From my days with Virginie at The Brio, to working with Malindi and becoming more established professionally, I appreciate all of the kind souls that helped me along the way.

To my new friends on TikTok, Instagram and Youtube, thank you for your continuous support. And to my friends who were there before the followers, thank you for sticking with me. You all make creating content that much more fun and rewarding for me.

And finally, thank you to my family back home, notably my Nana, that still doesn't understand what social media is but cheers me on from afar.

About Me

I moved to Paris in 2017 on what was supposed to be a study abroad semester and simply, never left. I've spent these last four years studying French, working in Real Estate, and most recently, creating content about life in Paris! My path from studying Architecture at Columbia to living in Paris has not been traditional (or well thought out). I've had to figure a lot of things out as I go which is why I am here to share my experiences, tips and tricks, and funny stories.

A FRIENDLY REMINDER: I'VE DONE MY RESEARCH, BUT YOU SHOULD TOO! CHECK MY SOURCES AGAINST YOUR OWN, AND ALWAYS EXERCISE SOUND JUDGEMENT.

Let's stay connected// À Bientôt

|

Website : www.kianatiese.com

Instagram : @chief_kii

Tik Tok : @kianatiese

Youtube : Kiana Tiese

Things I wish I knew Before Moving to *Paris*

A quick workbook by Kiana Tiese

New City, New You

Paris is a city known for romance and also highly romanticized. Before beginning the process (applying for your visa, looking for apartments, buying flights), its's always good to be sure of your 'why'.

Why Paris?

_____
_____
_____
_____
_____
_____
_____

Why Now?

_____
_____
_____
_____
_____
_____
_____

Keep this page and take a look at it before every visa renewal or administrative task.

First Week Things

PICTURES   Take photo booth pictures in the subway stations.

RIDE   Use said pictures for your metro pass (Navigo).

SEE   Go to Sacré-Cœur Basilica at sundown to see the city glow.

COPY   Make copies of your important documents. There are Office Depots here.

WRITE   Take notes of everything you see and try and your first impressions.

Things you may need

If you're anything like me, organization is not your strong suit. Are there any tasks you **need** to complete before moving? List them here:

_____

- [ ] Adaptor for your electronics
- [ ] Walking shoes
- [ ] Portable charger
- [ ] Medical prescriptions
- [ ] Lined paper journal
- [ ] Seasonings (ranch mix, cajun, etc)
- [ ] Feminine items (they have different brands here)

- [ ] _____
- [ ] _____
- [ ] _____
- [ ] _____
- [ ] _____
- [ ] _____
- [ ] _____

Don't pack too heavily because you can find all that you need here. Also, keep in mind the average apartment size in Paris may be smaller than what you are used to. You may have to downsize.

Apartment Hunting

Left bank, Right bank, Central? What's the right fit for you?

Technically, the Left and Right bank are split along the Seine River. The Left Bank is above the Seine and the Right Bank is below. But naturally, as an Anglophone, I think of Left and Right as West and East.

☐	TRENDY	☐	HISTORICAL	☐	HIPSTER	☐	NIGHTLIFE
☐	UPSCALE	☐	EASY TO REACH	☐	DIVERSE	☐	AFFORDABLE
☐	RESIDENTIAL	☐	STUDENT LIFE	☐	STREET FOOD	☐	VILLAGE-LIKE
☐	TOURISTY AREAS	☐	ENGLISH SPEAKERS	☐	STREET ART	☐	ARTSY

if you chose more on the left, check out these arrondissements:

18, 17, 16, 8, 7, 15, 14

if you chose more in the center, check out these arrondissements:

1, 2, 3, 4, 5, 6, 9

if you chose more on the right, check out these arrondissements:

19, 20, 10, 11, 12, 13

I've lived in the 18th, 14th, 9th, 11th and close suburbs. I suggest visiting your desired neighborhoods at different times of day, weekends etc., to see if you like the vibe of your part of the arrondissement.

Anyone hungry?

You may be dreaming of baguettes, croissants, macaroons, brie cheese and eclairs, I know I was! My first weeks in Paris were very wine, cheese and dessert heavy. No shame in it!

FILL IN YOUR PARIS GROCERY LIST

wine	cheese	pâtisserie

You can find great wine in local supermarkets, great cheese in Fromageries and pâtisserie on any street corner. Here are some of my favorites:

CHABLIS	COMTÉ	MADELEINE
CÔTES DU RHÔNE	CAMEMBERT	MILLE-FEUILLES
CHINON	CHEVRE	TARTE TATIN
	CANTAL	TARTE AUX FRAISE
	ROQUEFORT	

What Are You Bringing?

Showing up to someone's apéritif empty-handed is a big no-no in Paris! No need to go all out, but do stop by the market before going upstairs and pick up a few treats!

☐ JAMBON	☐ CHEESE CUBES	☐ TARAMA	☐ CHERRY TOMATOES
☐ CHARCUTERIE MEAT	☐ CHEVRE	☐ RILLETTES DU THON	☐ HUMMUS
☐ CROQUETTAS	☐ CAMEMBERT	☐ BATTONETS CRABE	☐ GUACAMOLE
☐ OLIVES	☐ COMTE	☐ TARTINABLE CREVETTES	☐ TZATZIKI
SALTY	CHEESEY	FISHY	FRESH

Bring a backup baguette in case someone else forgot to. Also, a bottle of anything is always appreciated!

Favorite places to visit

MUSEUM	Musee d'Orsay
CAFE	Broken Biscuits, KB Cafe
PARK	Parc des Buttes Chaumont
CHOCOLATIER	Alain Ducasse
VIEWS OF PARIS	Printemps Haussmann
PLACE TO MEET PEOPLE	Canal St. Martin
COCKTAILS	Octopus bar, le Perchoir, Jacques bar
TREAT	Popelini

Your Paris bucket-list

ARTS

FOOD

ENTERTAINMENT

LEARN

Thank you //Merci!

If you enjoyed this ebook and workbook please let me and the world know!

@KIANATIESE

see you in Paris!

Made in the USA
Monee, IL
26 November 2022